Fact Finders®

DISCOVER EARTH SCIENCE

LIQUID PLANET

Exploring Water on Earth with
SCIENCE PROJECTS

by Tammy Enz

Consultant:
Ginger L. Schmid, PhD, Associate Professor
Department of Geography
Minnesota State University, Mankato

CAPSTONE PRESS
a capstone imprint

Fact Finders Books are published by Capstone Press,
1710 Roe Crest Drive, North Mankato, Minnesota 56003
www.capstonepub.com

Library of Congress Cataloging-in-Publication Data
Enz, Tammy, author.
  Liquid planet : exploring water on Earth with science projects / by Tammy Enz.
      pages cm.—(Fact finders. Discover Earth science)
  Summary: "Illustrated instructions for experiments pertaining to water on Earth,
including the water cycle, evaporation, transpiration, and precipitation"—Provided
by publisher.
  Includes bibliographical references and index.
  ISBN 978-1-4914-4817-5 (library binding)
  ISBN 978-1-4914-4916-5 (eBook PDF)
1. Water—Experiments—Juvenile literature. 2. Hydrology—Juvenile literature. 3.
Science projects—Juvenile literature. 4. Earth (Planet)—Experiments—Juvenile
literature. I. Title.
  GB662.3.E59 2016
  551.48078—dc23   2014050237

Editorial Credits
Alesha Sullivan, editor; Sarah Bennett, designer; Kelly Garvin, media researcher;
Lori Barbeau, production specialist

Photo Credits
Captstone Press/Karon Dubke, 8, 9, 11, 12, 13 (left), 15, 16–17, 18, 19, 21 (right), 25,
28; Shutterstock: Africa Studio, 10, alybaba, 12–13, bogdan ionescu, 20–21, chaoss,
29, Charles Knowles, 22–23, EpicStockMedia, 26, ifong, 14, Jose Ignacio Soto, 6–7,
Justin Black, 4–5, Maksym Darakchi, 17 (top inset), MarArt, 23, O.Guero, cover,
stockshoppe, 7 (inset), violetkaipa, 27

Design Elements: Shutterstock: Curly Pat, Magnia, Markovka, Ms.Moloko, Orfeev,
pockygallery, Sashatigar

Printed in the United States of America in Stevens Point, Wisconsin.
032015   008824WZF15

Table of Contents

Water on Earth 4

Experiment 1
Sun, Earth, and Water 6

Experiment 2
A Disappearing Act 10

Experiment 3
Hardworking Plants 14

Experiment 4
Clouds and Condensation 16

Experiment 5
Shimmering Rainbow 20

Experiment 6
Incredible Edible Aquifer 22

Experiment 7
Make Your Own Drinking Water 26

Glossary 30
Read More 31
Internet Sites 31
Index 32

Water on Earth

Can you imagine our planet without any water? There would be no summertime dips in the pool. You couldn't enjoy a refreshing glass of water after a day of playing at the park. But that's not all. Without water Earth would be a very different planet.

Most of Earth's surface is covered with water. But you'll also find water in the air, under the ground, in lakes and rivers, and even inside of you. Scientists are busily searching the solar system for signs of water on other planets. Why? Life can only exist where there is water. So far Earth is the only planet where water is known to exist.

Did you know water is more than just a liquid? Water is solid when it becomes ice. As water **vapor** it is an invisible gas floating around the **atmosphere**. Want to get an up-close look at water's role on Earth? Grab some supplies and dive into experiments that will teach you all about water! You may need an adult's help for some—think safety first!

vapor–a gas made from something that is usually a liquid or solid at normal temperatures

atmosphere–the mixture of gases that surrounds Earth

Sun, Earth, and Water

Water is found in obvious places, such as rivers and oceans. But did you know water is also inside plants and clouds? Water even forms pools in giant caves underground.

Water is constantly moving and changing its form. How does this moving and changing take place? Lots of processes are involved, such as the **water cycle**. With a few materials you can see how this cycle moves water between Earth and the sky.

water cycle–how water changes as it travels around the world and moves between the ground and the air

The Water Cycle

Liquid water enters the atmosphere through **evaporation** or **transpiration**. In transpiration plants breathe out water vapor. The gaseous water cools in the air and **condenses** into clouds. When the clouds have gathered enough heavy water droplets, **precipitation** falls to the ground. Precipitation can be in the form of rain, snow, or ice. Precipitation filters into the ground or runs into rivers and lakes. The water cycle process repeats over and over.

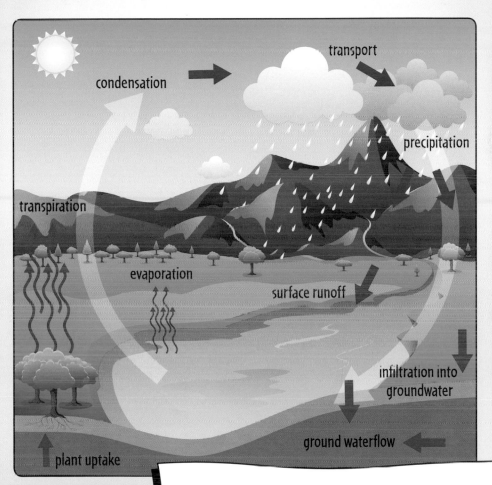

evaporate—to change from a liquid to a vapor or a gas
transpiration—the process by which plants give off moisture into the atmosphere
condense—to change from a gas to a liquid
precipitation—water that falls from clouds to Earth's surface

What You Do

1. Put 1 inch (2.5 cm) sand in the bottom of a plastic container.

2. Slowly pour water over the sand until the sand is damp. Stop pouring water when the sand no longer soaks up water. The sand represents Earth's surface.

3. Set a glass upright in the middle of the sand. Push it down into the sand.

What You Need

sand

plastic container the size of a shoe box

water

small glass at least 1 inch (2.5 centimeters) shorter than the plastic container

plastic wrap

tape

ice cubes

small dish

clock or timer

4. Cover the container with plastic wrap. Tape the plastic wrap securely to the sides of the container. The plastic wrap should be as airtight as possible. The plastic wrap represents Earth's atmosphere.

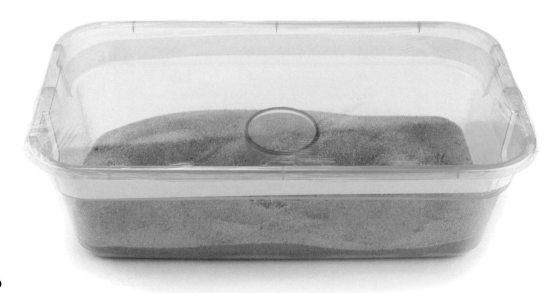

8

5. Place two or three ice cubes in a dish. Set the dish on the plastic wrap directly over the glass. Make sure there is a gap between the top of the glass and the bottom of the dish.

Helpful Hint: If the dish touches the glass, try to adjust the plastic wrap so it's tighter around the container.

6. Set the container in the sun for 30 minutes until the ice in the dish melts.

7. Carefully remove the dish and the plastic wrap. Look inside the glass. What do you see? Where did the water move? Did the sun's heat evaporate the water from the sand? You have created a simple water cycle!

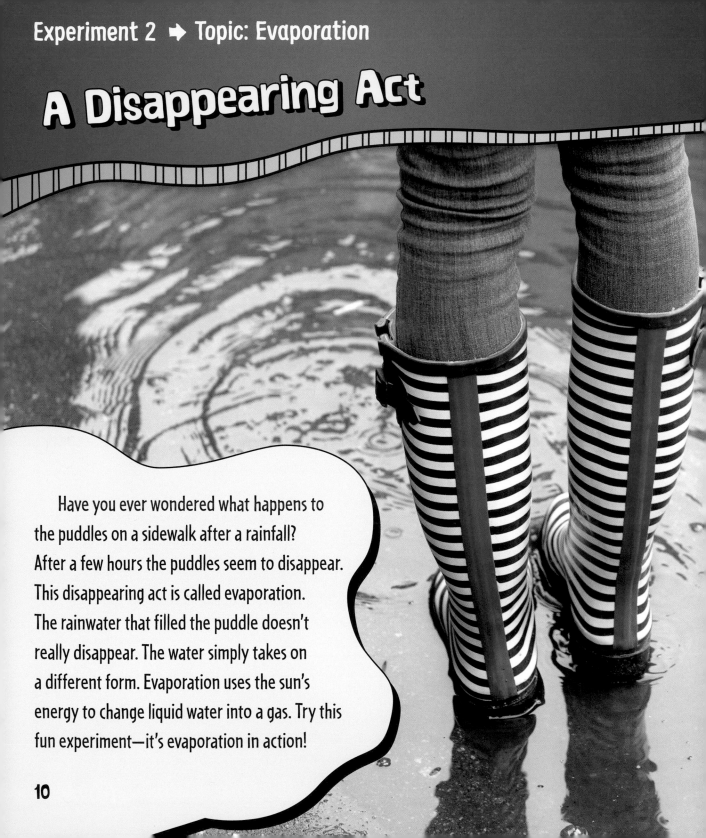

A Disappearing Act

Have you ever wondered what happens to the puddles on a sidewalk after a rainfall? After a few hours the puddles seem to disappear. This disappearing act is called evaporation. The rainwater that filled the puddle doesn't really disappear. The water simply takes on a different form. Evaporation uses the sun's energy to change liquid water into a gas. Try this fun experiment—it's evaporation in action!

Sweat Much?

Evaporation doesn't only happen to water on Earth. Water evaporates from you too. Sweating is an amazing process that helps keep you cool. When your body sweats, the evaporation of the sweat droplets pulls heat away from your body, lowering your temperature. Dogs also sweat, but they have a different way of cooling down. On top of sweating from their footpads, they pant. Panting causes water to evaporate off their tongues.

What You Need

3 identical sponges

bucket of water

3 plastic plates

electric fan

electric hair dryer

clock or timer

What You Do

1. Soak the sponges in a bucket of water. Pull each sponge out, and gently squeeze until no water drips out. The sponges should be damp.

2. Place each sponge on the center of a plate.

3. Set one plate indoors in a place it won't be disturbed.

4. Place the second plate in front of a fan. Set the fan to the lowest setting.

5. Carefully blow heat on the third plate. The hair dryer should be on the lowest heat setting.

6. Using a timer, keep track of how long it takes for each sponge to completely dry. Which sponge dries the fastest? Which dries the slowest?

Helpful Hint: The heat from the hair dryer mimics the sun's heat.

Hardworking Plants

Evaporation isn't the only process that changes liquid water into gaseous water. Transpiration is a cycle too. Plant roots pull water from the ground. Tiny pores on the leaves called stomata release gaseous water vapor into the air. Try this simple experiment to see how transpiration works.

FACT

Transpiration is often an invisible process. An acre (0.4 hectare) of corn contributes 3,000 to 4,000 gallons (11,400 to 15,100 liters) of water into the atmosphere each day. A large tree can transpire 40,000 gallons (151,400 liters) of water per year!

What You Need

small potted plant

plastic wrap

twist tie

petroleum jelly

glass jar

timer or clock

What You Do

1. Cover the pot, the soil, and the base of the plant with plastic wrap. Make sure it is as airtight as possible. Do not wrap the plant itself.

2. Use the twist tie to hold the plastic wrap tightly to the plant's stem.

3. Smear petroleum jelly around the rim of the jar's mouth. Carefully place the jar upside down over the plant. Push against the plastic wrap to form a tight seal.

4. Set the plant in the sun. Observe the plant for 30 to 60 minutes. What do you notice happening inside the jar? Are there water droplets on the inside of the jar?

Clouds and Condensation

Water vapor in the atmosphere is the key ingredient of rainmaking clouds. But vapor isn't all that's needed. Vapor high in the atmosphere cools and becomes water drops. But what holds the droplets in the sky long enough to form a cloud?

The "glue" that helps the droplets form comes from tiny dust particles floating in the atmosphere. Droplets cling to the dust, which forms a cloud. When enough droplets gather together, they become heavy enough to drop to Earth as rain or snow. See how this process of condensation works with your own cloud-making experiment.

Types of Clouds

There are many types of clouds. **Stratus clouds** are low horizontal clouds that blanket the sky. Stratus clouds usually mean rain or snow is on the way. Puffy vertical clouds are called **cumulus clouds**. When they turn from white and puffy to dark gray, rain is likely looming. On a nice day you may see wispy **cirrus clouds**. They are formed from ice crystals high in the sky. **Nimbus clouds** have snow or rain falling from them. Clouds can also be combinations of various types. A cumulonimbus cloud, for example, is a puffy cloud with rain falling from it.

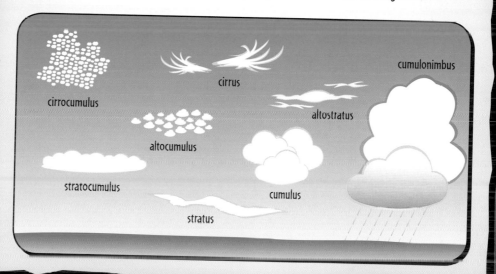

stratus cloud—a low cloud that forms over a large area; stratus clouds often bring light rain

cumulus cloud—a white, puffy cloud with a flat, rounded base

cirrus cloud—a high, thin cloud made of ice crystals that looks like strands of white silk

nimbus cloud—a cloud that produces precipitation

What You Do

1. Pour hot water into a jar until the water is about 1 inch (2.5 cm) high. Swish it around to warm the inside of the jar.

2. Place two ice cubes in the jar's upside-down lid. Place the upside-down lid with the ice cubes in it on top of the jar.

3. Hold a piece of dark paper behind the jar. This will help you see condensation beginning to form on the jar.

4. Have an adult light the matches while you lift the lid off the jar. Have the adult toss the matches into the jar. Quickly put the lid back on the jar.

5. With the dark paper in place, watch a swirling cloud begin to form! How do you think the cloud formed? Where do you see condensation?

Shimmering Rainbow

The water that collects in clouds eventually becomes raindrops or snowflakes. Sometimes when conditions are right, this precipitation in the air gives us an amazing display, such as a rainbow. As sunlight passes through raindrops, the light slows down and bends. The **wavelengths** of light separate into rainbow colors. But you don't have to wait for a rain shower to see a rainbow. Follow these steps to create your own!

20

wavelength–the distance between two peaks of a wave of light or sound

What You Do

1. Place a small mirror inside a glass. Lean the mirror against one side of the glass so it is slightly angled.

2. Fill the glass with water until the mirror is completely underwater.

3. Put the glass on the floor in a very dark room. Make sure all outside light is blocked.

4. Shine a flashlight through the glass at a slight angle from the mirror. Where do you see a rainbow?

What You Need

small mirror

glass large enough to fit the mirror inside

water

flashlight

ROY G. BIV

When you see a rainbow, it looks like a giant arch. But a rainbow is actually a complete circle. If conditions are right, you can see a complete rainbow from an airplane. You'll always see the color red on the outer edge of a rainbow. Red is the color with the longest wavelength. Red is followed by orange, yellow, green, blue, indigo, and then violet. The name ROY G. BIV can be used to help remember the first letter of each of the colors in order.

21

Incredible Edible Aquifer

Some rain finds its way to streams and rivers and is eventually carried to the ocean. But some rain seeps into the ground where it fills underground **aquifers**. The water is cleaned by the soil and stored underground. Some of the water is pumped to the surface and is used as drinking water. With this project you can build your own aquifer—and eat it too!

22

aquifer—underground area where water fills up space between rocks and sediment

Aquifer

Aquifers are a great source for fresh drinking water and for crop irrigation. In the form of precipitation, water can re-enter an aquifer to refill its empty spaces.

What You Do

What You Need

large, clear glass

small gummy bears

chocolate chips

crushed ice cubes

clear lemon-lime soda

ice cream

sprinkles

drinking straw

1. Fill a clear glass ⅓ full with a combination of gummy bears, chocolate chips, and crushed ice. These small items represent soil and dirt that make up an aquifer.

2. Add clear soda until the gummy bears, chocolate chips, and crushed ice are covered. The soda is groundwater and fills the spaces between the soil and rocks.

3. Add a scoop of ice cream to the cup. The ice cream is a **confining layer** above the aquifer and protects the water from being contaminated.

4. Pour sprinkles on top of the ice cream. The sprinkles represent soil, which is **porous** and allows water to seep through.

5. "Drill" a **well** into your aquifer with a straw. Begin to pump the well by slowly sucking on the straw. What happens to the soda groundwater?

6. Recharge the aquifer by adding a little more soda, also known as precipitation. Where does the soda go?

confining layer–a layer of rock or clay between Earth's surface and an underground aquifer; water does not easily seep through a confining layer

porous–having tiny holes through which gas or liquid may pass through

well–a deep hole sunk into the ground to obtain water

Make Your Own Drinking Water

Is it possible for Earth to run out of drinking water? Safe drinking water is in short supply in many places on Earth. One reason is that most of the water on the planet is salty ocean water. Humans cannot drink salt water. But a simple tool based on a natural process can make salt water drinkable. Try this **desalination** project for yourself.

desalinate—the process of removing salt from water

What You Do

1. Pour 4 cups (1 liter) water into a mixing bowl.

2. Add 2 tablespoons (30 grams) salt, and stir with the spoon until the salt is dissolved in the water. Dip a clean finger in the salty water, and taste it.

Helpful Hint: Make sure all supplies used in this project are clean and sanitary.

3. Place a drinking glass inside the bowl, and center the glass in the bowl.

4. Stretch plastic wrap over the bowl. Make sure the top of the bowl is completely covered and the wrap is tightly sealed to the bowl.

5. Place a rock on the plastic wrap directly over the cup. Make sure the plastic wrap doesn't touch the top of the glass.

6. Place the bowl in the sun or under an incandescent lamp for two hours.

7. Carefully remove the rock and the plastic wrap. Remove the drinking glass and taste the water inside it. Does the water taste salty?

The Most Important Liquid on the Planet

Water is the most precious and life-sustaining resource on Earth. Without it life could not exist. Next time you drink a glass of water, think about all the places it has been. Think of all the ways it plays a role in your life. And think of the fun you had while experimenting with Earth's natural processes dealing with water!

Glossary

aquifer (AK-wuh-fuhr)– underground area where water fills up space between rocks and sediment

atmosphere (AT-muh-sfeer)–the mixture of gases that surrounds Earth

cirrus cloud (SEER-uhs KLOWD)–a high, thin cloud made of ice crystals that looks like strands of white silk

condense (kuhn-DENS)–to change from a gas to a liquid

confining layer (KON-fine-ing LAY-ur)–a layer of rock or clay between Earth's surface and an underground aquifer; water does not easily seep through a confining layer

cumulus cloud (KYOO-myuh-luhs KLOWD)–a white, puffy cloud with a flat, rounded base

desalinate (dee-SAL-uh-neyt)–the process of removing salt from water

evaporate (i-VA-puh-rayt)–to change from a liquid to a vapor or a gas

nimbus cloud (NIM-buhss KLOWD)–a cloud that produces precipitation

porous (POR-uhss)–having tiny holes through which gas or liquid may pass through

precipitation (pri-sip-i-TAY-shuhn)–water that falls from clouds to Earth's surface

stratus cloud (STRA-tuhss KLOWD)–a low cloud that forms over a large area; stratus clouds often bring light rain

transpiration (transs-puh-RAY-shuhn)–the process by which plants give off moisture into the atmosphere

vapor (VAY-pur)–a gas made from something that is usually a liquid or solid at normal temperatures

water cycle (WAH-tur SY-kuhl)–how water changes as it travels around the world and moves between the ground and the air

wavelength (WAYV-length)–the distance between two peaks of a wave of light or sound

well (WEL)–a deep hole sunk into the ground to obtain water

Read More

Beatty, Richard. *Rivers, Lakes, Streams, and Ponds.* Biomes Atlases.
Chicago: Raintree, 2011.

Mulder, Michelle. *Every Last Drop: Bringing Clean Water Home.* Orca Footprints.
Custer, Wash.: Orca Book Publishers, 2014.

Oxlade, Chris. *Experiments with Air and Water.* Excellent Science Experiments.
New York: PowerKids Press, 2015.

Internet Sites

FactHound offers a safe, fun way to find Internet sites related to this book.
All of the sites on FactHound have been researched by our staff.

Here's all you do:
Visit *www.facthound.com*
Type in this code: **9781491448175**

 Check out projects, games and lots more at
www.capstonekids.com

Index

aquifers, 22, 23, 24
atmosphere, 4, 7, 8, 14, 16

caves, 6
clouds, 6, 7, 16, 17, 19, 20
clouds, types of
    cirrus, 17
    cumulus, 17
    nimbus, 17
    stratus, 17
condensation, 7, 16, 18

desalination, 26

evaporation, 7, 9, 10, 11, 14

freshwater, 23, 27

gases, 4, 7, 10, 14
glaciers, 27

lakes, 4, 7

oceans, 6, 22, 26

perspiration, 11
plants, 6, 7, 14, 15
precipitation, 7, 20, 23, 24

rain, 7, 10, 16, 17, 20, 22
rainbows, 20, 21
rivers, 4, 6, 7, 22

salt water, 26, 28
scientists, 4
snow, 7, 16, 17, 20
stomata, 14
streams, 22

transpiration, 7, 14

water cycle, 6, 7, 9, 14
water vapor, 4, 7, 14, 16
wavelengths, 20, 21